THE CUTTING

Maureen O'Brien

THE CUTTING

OBERON BOOKS
LONDON

First published in 2003 by Oberon Books Ltd.
(incorporating Absolute Classics)
521 Caledonian Road, London N7 9RH
Tel: 020 7607 3637 / Fax: 020 7607 3629
e-mail: oberon.books@btinternet.com
www.oberonbooks.com

A catalogue record for this book is available from the British
Library.

ISBN: 1 84002 321 X

Cover design: Andrzej Klimowski

Printed in Great Britain by Antony Rowe Ltd, Chippenham.

Characters

ALEX
a child psychiatrist, mid-forties

JUDITH
an only child, thirties

The Setting

Minimal. No clutter. Naturalism neither necessary nor desirable. The window can be painted, suspended, or simply created by a lighting effect, the carpet and chair also, to achieve the precise type of nastiness favoured by the production.

Lighting

Of supreme importance, to be used to change rhythm as well as to change scene.

Alex's Area

To be defined by a small harsh pool of light.

Judith's Cell

To be defined by a diagonal shaft of light.

Note

The play is not about two people battling for power. Nor is it a celebration of madness. It is about the struggle of one person to save the soul of another, and the emergence, through that struggle, of the possibility of a possibility of a life, and of a friendship.

Alex says 'Ach' once or twice. German origin is not to be inferred from this; it simply implies a harsher sound than 'Ah'.

It has been suggested that Alex could as well be played by a woman. On page 12 Mr would become Mrs, and on page 73, Judith would say *Alice* instead of *Alec*.

Scene 1

Darkness.

Desk lamp snaps on.

ALEX at desk, leafs through a bundle of newspaper cuttings held together by a bulldog clip.

Starts to read some. Can't look at others. Has done this before.

Thrusts them away with revulsion.

ALEX: Ah no.

No.

No.

No.

The light snaps out. In darkness:

a heavy iron door clangs shut.

Footsteps echo on stone floor.

On tape: Distant shouts of women, pots clattering, running footsteps, ALEX's breathing in darkness – acute fear. In prison for the first time, sounds as though he has been running, though has not. Speech whispered and fast, in darkness on tape:

How did I get here?

What am I doing here?

And the warders. Screws, whatever you call them.

Breath or laugh.

Someone has to do the job I suppose.

Scene 2

A light comes up on ALEX and follows him waveringly like a torch. He appears and disappears. The effect confusion, disorientation.

ALEX: One of them conducted me to the – cell – where I was instructed to peer through a spy hole.
I know we observe the children at the clinic. We need to. This however sickens me.
I feel like a spy.

JUDITH: (*Revealed in a diagonal shaft of light from high up.*

She sits on a bed or bench (undefined). She is looking away from ALEX up towards the 'window'. Hands in her lap. An irretrievable air of tragedy. Long straight body. Long straight legs. Long dark face. Dark hair.

The two areas of light are separate. JUDITH and ALEX should not be separated by a 'real' door but by an area of darkness.)

ALEX: Perhaps because of the woman herself in that narrow room. She's like someone at a bus stop who has stopped waiting.
You see children taken into so-called care. They sit. Like her. They don't wait. They just sit.

I watched her for fifty minutes. She didn't move.
Except once.

JUDITH: (*Turns her head towards ALEX. The rest of her body stays still. They seem to stare at each other. A moment of pure silence. Then a whisper:*)

ALEX: I expected a monster, Barratt.

I swear she stared straight into my eye.
She couldn't. She didn't know I was there.
There was a heavy door between us for Christsake.

JUDITH: (*Turns back to look at the high window.*)

ALEX: Then I was released.

Blackout on JUDITH.

In darkness:

Look, I didn't like this case when I read about it first and I like it no better now.
I – will – not – be – involved!

Blackout on ALEX.

Scene 3

ALEX snaps on his desk lamp. On the desk is a pocket recorder on which he has been listening to his voice.

ALEX: Yes, well. Wipe all that.

He fastwinds back. High pitched gobbledygook of tape. He holds Barratt's letter. Speaks into recorder.

Letter to Doctor Leo Barratt. Date etcetera, Dear Barratt.

Okay.

Dear Barratt.
Thanks for arranging the visit. The answer's still no. However, here are my brief observations for what they're worth. See why you at first thought waxy flexibility, suspected catatonia; but agree it's not that. I'd have said depressive stupor until – Something about her movement. And the eyes – there's a light there – Delete that. I agree, impossible to say whether the mutism is hysterical or elective. So you see, I've been as little use to you as I predicted. And can be of no further use I'm afraid. Terribly busy, colossal work-load as always. And no reason to suppose my methods might work where yours have failed – Delete that – Where yours have not

yet succeeded. Mutism doesn't respond to treatment. You know that. Even in children. They grow out of it. If you're lucky. And Autistic Aloneness is something else. My success with that is meaningless here. Not relevant. I haven't worked with adults in fifteen years. From choice. I work with children. With children there's hope. Leave me alone, Barratt! Delete that.

Looking at Barratt's letter:

What do you think I'm going to do? Surround her with dolls and toys and sand-and-water play? The prison authorities would love that I'm sure. My 'flexible approach' as you put it has no more chance than the boringly orthodox. Like yours. I see why people are getting impatient. Five months is a long time. But time and patience are all you've got. In the meantime you're just going to have to say Unfit To Plead. What's wrong with that?

He turns over Barratt's letter. Reads.

Light up on JUDITH as before. She turns her head.

Blackout on JUDITH.

Ach.
Don't abreact her. Don't do that. Yes she might respond to I.V. Valium but she'll return to muteness afterwards. They always do. And anything she said on medication surely wouldn't stand up in court? Don't abreact her, old friend.

Ach. Damn.
Letter to Barratt.
Arrange for a new medical and a CAT Scan.
Send me the reports.

And get me a room away from the psychiatric wing.
Damn.

Scene 4

The room.

A door and a window.

An 'easy' chair of cheap design. A desk or table with a hard chair. A nasty piece of carpet with clashing colours.

JUDITH stands at the window, completely still.

The door opens. She does not move.

ALEX: Ah.
Yes.
Thank you.
Er.

> *The door closes in his face.*

Ah.
Good morning.
Judith?

JUDITH: (*Remains still.*)

ALEX: I'm Alex Dodd.

Your – Doctor Barratt arranged for me to come and for you and me to spend some time together. As I'm sure he explained.

I hope you're here – of your own free will? I shouldn't like to think you had been – coerced in any way?

I'm sorry you've been subjected to yet another medical examination. It's a requirement I'm afraid when a new – person – comes on the scene.

Would you like to sit down?

JUDITH: (*As before.*)

ALEX: Of course, not if you don't wish.

JUDITH: (*As before.*)

ALEX: I'm almost as new to prison as you are. I must admit
I'm shocked. It must be – hard for you? I've seen your –
cell.
Well at least this room is not so bad, is it? I mean it's not
so bad compared with –
Yes, it's awful, isn't it?
But a window you can see out of at least.
And you're even allowed to smoke!

Yes, if your window were wider I'd join you at it. If you'd
let me. But ugliness is the curse of our age, don't you
think? Not just of our public institutions.

Do you? Smoke?
I could bring you some cigarettes if you – I don't smoke
myself any longer. Sometimes, I have to admit, I wish I
still did.

What do you see out of your window?

JUDITH: (*As before.*)

ALEX: Judith –
Do you mind if I call you Judith?
I work with children a good deal and there we're always
on first name terms.
Oh.
Except for one small boy. His mother introduced me to
him as Mr Dodd and ever since he has addressed me as
Mr God. So, to avoid such confusions, I hope you'll call
me Alex?

JUDITH: (*As before.*)

ALEX: Anyway, Judith, this room, such as it is, is yours.
Your room. You can do in it whatever you please. For
one hour. Three times a week. We will do whatever you
want. You decide. If you want simply to stand and look

out of the window for an hour that's fine. If you want to
sit down for some of the time that's fine too.

I also want to say this to you. I am not here to – help the
police with their enquiries as it were. I am here for your
sake only. I've made that clear. To everyone concerned.
If you should ever feel compelled to speak to me, what
you say remains between us. Unless you decide
otherwise. That's my solemn promise. I work with
children. With children you don't break your word. I
won't break mine. There's no reason on earth why you
should believe me. I daresay you won't. It doesn't matter.
I tell you for what it's worth.
In this room, for three hours a week, you will be safe.
You will be in charge.

Lights fade down, then up.

JUDITH: (*As before.*)

ALEX at the table.

Silence for some time.

ALEX looks at his watch.

ALEX: We have five minutes more.

Silence.

I just want to say to you just one more thing. I know
you've been questioned and talked at and questioned
again. I'm just another mosquito buzzing in your ear. I'll
say this then shut up.
Judith, your silence. Your silence itself.
I'm not concerned with the criminal justice system, I'm
not concerned with whether you are guilty or innocent.
Those words mean very little to me. We are all guilty.
We are all innocent. I am only concerned to guide you
back – to help you begin the return journey so to speak
– should you want to make that journey. It's normal for

me to work with those who have found a refuge in silence.

A refuge though can also be a prison. Can't it? Silence can be a sort of – maze? You get yourself in so far that you can no longer find the way out. In your case, you see, a double imprisonment. What was I saying? Yes. I have helped many children to find their way out. Children who have made their den, their – lair, in silence. I have been the other end of the string.

That's why me. I am here for that. Should you want me for that.

That's all I wanted to say.

Oh, just one more thing.
Judith?
Are your eyes open? Or closed?

Blackout.

Scene 5

ALEX at his desk. Absorbed in letters clipped together. He is moved.

His voice on tape.

ALEX: I enclose my notes on the first sessions. I don't – as you'll see – hold out much hope.

I'm working my way through the informants' reports. A mountain. I'm scaling it. Inch by baffling inch.

He rubs his face. Pause.

Switches to 'record'.

Speaks to recorder.

Thanks for the copies of the letters. I've glanced at them. How unspeakably sad if, as you think, and I'm inclined to agree, they were written to an imaginary man.

Thanks also for the transcripts of police interviews. Time presses. But I'll get through them before my next – meeting with her.

Turns off recorder.

Still absorbed in letters.

Yes.

Blackout.

Scene 6

The room.

Bright light.

JUDITH stands as before.

The door is opened for ALEX to come in.

ALEX: Ah.
   Oh.
   Thank you.
   Yes.

   The door closes.

   Oh those women.
   I've made arrangements by the way. She'll stay outside only a few minutes, then go and – amuse – herself elsewhere. After that till the end of our – session – we are on our own. We won't be – overheard.
   They seemed to fear some danger. To me, I think. I assured them there was none.
   Good.
   You have come.
   I'm glad.
   Even if you are only here because it makes a change from your usual four walls. And because it has a window through which one can actually see.

How is your view today?

Silence.

No use asking if you'd like to sit down, I suppose?

No. Thought not.

You know, one thing you can't tell from looking so intently out of your window is that it's the most glorious spring day today. Impossible to tell that from your two square feet of sky.

Yes, I do keep mentioning the outside world to you. It's important that you continue to believe it exists. Most important. Please don't forget that it is still there. It would be easy for you to forget.
The whole world is not – like this.

Does the solitary confinement bother you?
They tell me they have done it for your own protection.
I hope you understand that. It is not meant as some kind of – extra punishment.
Punishment! You've not even been tried yet. No one has any idea what actually happened and yet – Here you are.

He settles down.

I have some questions for you today.
Are you bored with questions?
Aren't you bored?
The questions are for you, though I too would like to know the answers to them.
They're just for you.
To think about.

Am I real?
Judith?

Are you?

Is the window real?

And what you see outside the window. Is that real?

If I had us moved out of here to a room without a window? What would you do then? Even I might prove a more fascinating vista than a blank wall. Don't worry, it's not a threat. The window is yours. I won't take it away from you.
It's my present to you.

Is there anything else I could get for you?
That's a question I would like an answer to.

Another question for you: Do you know where you are?

You're in prison, Judith.
Do you know why?

Are these questions bothering you?

If you had three wishes, what would they be?

Would the first one be that I should shut up and go away?
All right, I'll shut up. In a minute.
But I won't go away.

Blackout.

ALEX's voice in darkness:

I'm going to read you something today. Something about yourself.

Scene 7

The room.

Bright light.

JUDITH as before.

ALEX with much paper.

ALEX: Judith?

> Do you mind?
> Stop me if it bothers you.
> I won't read anything against your will.
> See this mountain of paper?
> This is you.
> Things said. About you.
> So you see you are real to others. More real than you are to yourself?
> More real than others are to you?

> Reports.
> Reports.
> Reports.
> School reports. Medical reports. Police reports.

> I'm going to read – this.
> Tell me if you disagree with anything it says.
> Other people's views of us generally strike us as – odd, to say the least.
> School. Look at this. You were good at school. I guessed that, you know. Especially good in Art. The Art teacher over and over: 'Excellent work', 'Unusual talent', 'I have great hopes of Judith'.

> Judith?

> The Art books I had left in your cell. You haven't touched them, they tell me. Except to turn the Impressionists onto their back. Rougher treatment than they deserve, I'd have thought?
> You were allowed only the books, I'm afraid. Paper and pencils were out of the question. And paint. Even finger paints. Have you ever done that, Judith? Finger painting? I do it often. Even for adults it can be fun –

> Fun.

> Yes. Well. Never mind.

Okay. Medical reports.
Is it true you never visited a doctor in the whole of your life?
Until your arrest. Remand.
Have you any idea how unusual that is?
Judith?

You've certainly made up for it since.

Okay. Now I'm on to police reports.
Are you fed up with this, Judith?
Am I driving you insane?

This is a transcript of an interview conducted by the police with one of the colleagues with whom you used to work. Her name is Betty.
And I'm going to read it to you whether you like it or not. All right?
Right.
Here we are.
They ask Betty how you normally seemed. She says you were 'Very quiet, like.'
Yes! Imagine, Judith!
'She came in, she smiled, she did her work, she went home. She'd say Yes No Please Thank you. But she never chatted like.'
It appears, Judith, you see, that your leaning towards silence is something not entirely new.
Hey?
What do you say to that?

Ah yes. Now.
Do you recall a person in the office by the name of Cheryl, by the way?

JUDITH: (*Makes an infinitesimal movement of the head.*)

A moment's silence.

ALEX: Apparently your quietness disturbed Cheryl. Betty says – Where are we? – Yes, Betty says, 'It used to get on

Cheryl's nerves some reason, Judith not talking like.
Cheryl started goading her. She didn't rise to it, Judith
didn't, she got quieter if anything. Then Cheryl seemed
to get sort of uncomfortable. She started coming in later
and later in the mornings and Mr Blake warned her
about it eventually and she told him where he could stuff
his whatsername job, oh excuse me but you know. And
she picked up her things and flounced out. That's the last
we saw of Cheryl.' Good work, Judith! But don't bank on
its working with me. I've a lot more staying power than
Cheryl, you know.

Yes.

Now Betty says you cheered up after that. 'She'd smile
again in the morning when she came in.' That's the limit
of Betty's power of description.

But you liked Betty, didn't you? I think I have proof that
you did.

Now listen. Here's a question the police didn't think to
ask. Where is it now? But Doctor Barratt asked it. Here
it is.

'Did any noticeable change come over Judith,' he asks
Betty, 'In, say, the last few weeks she was working here?'
'Well, we did start to think she was getting a bit odd
actually,' says Betty. 'She wouldn't hear if you spoke to
her. She didn't seem to know where she was hardly
sometimes. I started noticing it a couple of months
before she left. In the summer anyway.' Doctor Barratt
then wants to know how you came to leave. Here's Betty
again: 'Well, Mr Blake came through from his office with
some things for her to see to like, and he's standing by
her desk and she just didn't seem to know he was there
even. Mr Blake smiles, you know, and says, Oh I think
Judith must be in love! he says. And that was that. She
didn't come in the next day and then not the next. I went
up there to see if she was all right 'cause it wasn't like
her to stay off sick. I knocked and knocked but there was
no reply. So I put a little note through the door saying

Dear Judith, please let us know if you're all right and can I get you anything like. Then I went.'

'A few days later,' Betty says, 'Mr Blake told us she'd resigned.' But two weeks after that you went into the office and took with you a present for Betty. A book with lovely pictures.

Asked if she had ever met your mother, Betty says no, she didn't think anybody had: 'She never went out, her mother; never had; not for years. One of those phobia type of things I think it was.'

Your neighbours agree. 'They kept themselves to themselves' was the general view.

By the way, Betty liked the pictures so much she cut them out and framed them. They are hanging on her bedroom wall. How does that – grab you – as they say? Judith?

You'd hardly be pleased? I've seen the books in your house. They are wonderful books. Was it your mother who collected them?

Your father perhaps?

You?

That's quite a climb from Bedminster Parade. Over the Hill and up Saint Luke's Steps. She did it, though, Betty. In spite of her lack of artistic judgement. To see if you were all right. Were you there when she arrived?

Were you watching from a window? Hiding?

Your mother was still alive then. Wasn't she?

Were you sorry when she went away?

Betty.

Yes. A few weeks later you went down and gave her the book.

Judith!

You've had only one job in the whole of your life. You were there in that office with people who were fond of you and whom I believe you were fond of in return. For fifteen years. Fifteen years. The whole of your adult life.

Now something happened to you about two months before you left that job. Something that may have changed the whole course of that life. Some profoundly affecting event. What was it, Judith? What?

Silence. He waits. He looks at his watch. Starts to pack his things into his briefcase.

JUDITH turns from the window in such a way as to make it impossible for ALEX to see her face.

She walks slowly to the middle of the room.

She stands there with her back to ALEX. She puts her hands in her pockets and bends her head.

She stays like that. No one speaks.

The door opens.

JUDITH walks slowly to the door and goes out.

Blackout on ALEX's reaction.

In darkness: At ALEX's desk the sound of a bottle of scotch being opened. Scotch being poured into a glass. The bottle is put on the desk.

Scene 8

Desk light snaps on.

ALEX drinks and pours another.

He stands, laughs, drinks.

He turns, on the spot.

Laughs again. Drinks. Sits.

Speaks to recorder.

ALEX: Of course we could be back to square one again tomorrow.

Blackout.

Scene 9

The room.

Bright light.

The door closes behind ALEX as he enters.

We are not back to square one. JUDITH stands in the middle of the room, her back to the chair and to ALEX.

ALEX: Ah.

> You are in the sun.
> Even there, it – reaches you.
>
> Good.
>
> *He settles himself and his objects at the table.*
>
> I have a bulging briefcase today. Not full of you. My other cases. Children, all of them. Many in great distress, great darkness. One day I hope for my briefcase to be full of light.
> And then I'll be out of a job!
>
> From here one can almost believe that out there under that blue sky there was not a prison yard but grass, fields, trees. Do you know why? It's because the birds are singing.
>
> If I talk to you about your mother, will you mind?

JUDITH: (*Reacts.*)

ALEX: Ah.

> All right. No talk about your mother today.
>
> *He settles down.*
>
> The traffic was a – nuisance this morning. This room has started to seem like a haven of peace.

He laughs.

Of course I don't mean –

Well, never mind.

Now………

All right.

I'm going to ask you again about what happened in your life two months or so before you resigned from your job.

Judith?

Something happened –

JUDITH: (*Moves to the door keeping her back to ALEX. She beats on the door with her fists.*)

ALEX: Judith, are you sure you want to leave?

JUDITH: (*Beats harder on the door.*)

The door opens.

ALEX: I think somehow the answer to that is yes.

JUDITH: (*Goes out.*)

ALEX: Goodbye Judith.

Blackout.

In darkness: ALEX's voice on tape reverberates and fades:

Judith!

Scene 10

Desk light snaps on.

ALEX: That's it! I've found the key!
And I've blown it.
She's never going to come back.

He reaches for the whisky bottle and knocks the recorder to the floor.

Oh GOD!

He bends to pick it up.

He looks at it.

Blackout.

Scene 11

The room.

Grey day.

Door closes behind ALEX.

The chair has its back to him. The room appears empty. He has blown it?

JUDITH rises from the chair.

ALEX: (*Involuntary intake of breath.*)

JUDITH: (*Moves towards the window.*)

ALEX: Good morning, Judith.

Goes to his table without waiting for a reply. Brisk:

The rain it raineth but we have our decor to cheer us up.

He takes things from his briefcase, places them on the table. The last thing is the tape recorder.

I see you prefer the rain.
I can't say I blame you.

He speaks into the recorder.

There. We are ready. We speak into the ear of posterity.

He fastwinds back. Then plays: 'We speak into the ear of posterity.' switches to record.

Good. That's fine.

JUDITH: (*Turns.*)

> *Tremendous though short silence.*

ALEX: Ah!

> Yes, it's a tape recorder. I use it every evening to record my notes, as it were, on the day's work. Sometimes I record my patients as we go along.
> Do you mind?
> (*Into the recorder.*)
> Judith has shrugged and turned back to her window. She means what is the point of recording her silence? I think that is what she means?
>
> I am going to take her shrug of indifference for consent.
> (*To JUDITH:*)
> Yes? No objection?
>
> Very well.

> *Silence.*

> Shall I tell you why I find it useful to record even silence, Judith?
> Well, I will.
> You see, you stand there listening, I imagine, to your thoughts, your memories, your conjectures about the future perhaps, your fears, sadnesses, hopes, despairs. But.
> When I turn on this little machine and the tape starts whirring round; you know what you listen to then?
>
> You start to listen to your silence.
>
> The machine makes you hear it.
>
> You start to listen to the present moment passing. To your presence, as it were, in that present. This present. Do you see?
>
> Well, that's the general idea anyway.

Let's listen to it now, shall we?
Your silence.

He puts the recorder on the table.

No sound. Except perhaps distant noises: Traffic, clangs, pots, shouts. A dog barks? Then:

JUDITH: (*Turns.*)

ALEX: Judith has turned from the window.
She is crossing the room. She is coming towards me.
She has – you have – you have stopped. By the chair.
You are – Judith is – sitting in the chair.

Hello, Judith.

Light fades last on JUDITH.

Scene 12

Lights up.

The room.

JUDITH and ALEX as before.

Silence.

ALEX: We have five minutes more.

Silence.

Blackout. A mere blink.

Scene 13

Lights up.

The room.

As before.

ALEX: This is it, Judith. This is all there is from now on. Do you understand?
Until you break the silence it will remain intact. There will be nothing else.

Blackout.

In darkness ALEX's voice on tape:

Listen to it! Listen! Hear it?
Weeks of it! Weeks of her life!
And all I discover is that I am terrified of silence and that my patient is not!

She's – idling in neutral.
We're stuck.

Scene 14

Lights up.

The room.

As before.

Silence.

ALEX looks at his watch.

ALEX: We have five minutes more.

Short silence.

JUDITH: (*Stands.*)

Then walks to the window.

Stays there.

Blackout on ALEX's reaction.

In darkness ALEX's voice on tape:

ALEX: Aaaagh!

Scene 15

Desk lamp snaps on.

ALEX at desk continues the recorded sound of frustration.

He speaks into recorder.

ALEX: Three sessions ago she went back to the window.
I've lost her, Barratt. She's gone. She's gone.

You're listening to the sound of failure. This is it.

Lights fade.

Scene 16

Lights up.

The room.

JUDITH at the window.

ALEX discovered at the door still holding his briefcase. He deliberates before putting down briefcase and starting to speak.

ALEX: Judith.
I work day after day, year after year with sad, suffering, helpless children. They're like you, these children. They're just like you. They sit. They don't wait. Or hope. They've given that up long ago. Someone will eventually turn up to move them to another place on the road. They know that place will be no better and no worse than the place they are in. I have turned up in this place. But you

are not a child, and I have to tell you I no longer know how to proceed. I no longer know what I am here for. I haven't even managed to find out what on earth it is you want! Perhaps just to be left alone with whatever terrible, or, who knows, delicious thoughts make their macabre dance through your head

Look, as a doctor, it's my whole, my sole, my passion – a frenzy almost – to cure, to bring back from whatever, wherever, what – nightmare keeps my patients in the dark. But they have to want that too. And you don't, Judith.

I can see, of course I can see, that if you've done something as grotesque, as extraordinary as what you appear to have done – who knows since you refuse to say – that you'd see that as the end. What is possible after it? The rest is indeed silence. But I can't bear to see it, you understand? I have to give my time back where it is needed. I can't keep coming here to be a plaything in the sad little game you are playing with your life.

Do you hear what I'm saying, Judith? This is the end. Do you hear what I'm saying? For Godsake turn round from that empty window and look at me. What do you see from the thing? There's a wall. There are twelve blind windows, a square foot of sky, there's nothing there. What for heaven's sake do you see?

(*He groans.*)

Oh God. I'm sorry. I didn't mean. An outburst like that. Unprofessional. And cruel. I'm so sorry.

But the fact remains, I have to go. So this is it, Judith. I have to say goodbye.

Silence.

Doctor Barratt will be back to see you on Monday.

Silence.

Well. Goodbye.

Silence.

He goes to open the door.

It is locked.

Oh my God!

Pause.

I could 'activate the alarm', of course, and make a fuss.
But I shan't. So………

I'm imprisoned here. A forty minute jail sentence. So
this is how it feels. Oh what a farce.

*He starts to laugh. Goes back to table. Puts down his bag. His
laughter dies down.*

Ohhh, Lord. Jailed for professional misconduct. Quite
right too. Thoroughly deserved. Oh well……… All I can
do now, like you, is wait for my release.

He sits.

There is a truly embarrassed silence, not professional.

JUDITH: Trees.

ALEX: ………?

Judith?

JUDITH: What I see.

ALEX: Out of your window?

JUDITH: I see trees.

Blackout.

Interval.

Scene 17

Lights up.

The room.

JUDITH in the chair.

ALEX laying out his things on the table.

ALEX: Well, I don't have to invite you to sit today.
    You've washed your hair. It looks – very good.
    You're thin, you know.
    Were you always, even before – ?
    Or is it the notorious prison fare?
    I caught a glimpse of the lunch on my way in. It looked unspeakable.
    There.

He sits.

JUDITH: I'll speak – it.

ALEX: The lunch?

JUDITH: – little machine.

ALEX: Yes.
    Sure.

JUDITH: Is – working?

ALEX: It's working, yes. Yes, it's –

He shows her.

    It's working now.

JUDITH: – – very small machine.

ALEX: They are, these days.
    Judith.
    I was recording all the time. From the beginning.

JUDITH: Yes.

ALEX: You knew?

JUDITH: (*Looks at him.*)

ALEX: My God.

JUDITH: You're – optimist.

ALEX: I am, yes.
   Are you?

JUDITH: No.

ALEX: No.
   Can I bring us back to your mother?

JUDITH: Us?

ALEX: (*He takes that.*) You.

JUDITH: Do – have to?

ALEX: You are here because of your mother.

JUDITH: So are you.

ALEX: Me?

JUDITH: Because – of yours.

ALEX: Ha. And our fathers too of course. Let's not leave
   them out of it.

JUDITH: (*Bends her head.*)

ALEX: Does it distress you to talk about your mother?

JUDITH: No.

*The tape goes round. It is the only sound. JUDITH indicates
the recorder. She likes it:*

It – like – someone breathing.

ALEX: Who?

JUDITH: (*Laughs softly.*)

ALEX: Okay, no trick questions. Either my hearing is not as acute as yours or I am simply used to it. I can't hear it at all.

JUDITH: Hearing! Yes! Always! Always – – more! – – too much. Hearing. Too much. Quiet noise – loud. Loud noise – –– – knife in the head! Such pain! People doing such pain – – ! But why? Why ––– people – making – me such pain?

ALEX: People purposely cause you pain by the noise they make?

JUDITH: (*Shakes her head.*) No. Not – purpose. Not. – – not their fault. I hear more than –– –. – hear too much. – hear thoughts. I – hear – their – thoughts.

ALEX: Do they hear yours?

JUDITH: No. Hear my thoughts? No. Deaf. All deaf.

ALEX: How do you know?

JUDITH: – try. – –– experiments. – say a thing. – – think – different thing. – – see? They don't know. –– can't tell. –– don't – hear – my – thoughts.
Well, ––– – – appeared. – –– never ––– – sure.

ALEX: When you say you hear thoughts, do you mean voices? You hear them as voices?

JUDITH: Lonely. Isn't it? ––– no one to hear your thoughts? Talking – so much trouble. And –– – such chasms of misinterpretation.

ALEX: You are lonely? Would you say?

JUDITH: – wouldn't say. No.

ALEX: Without your mother? Were you close to her?

JUDITH: – – hear the birds today.

> – gulls loved it up there. – – –– – seaside. Before – opened –– eyes.

ALEX: Were you fond of the seaside?

JUDITH: – seaside? No. Never. Fond? No. Why – – – – –– – seaside?

ALEX: I suppose I thought it might lead us somewhere.

JUDITH: – only place – seaside leads – straight into the sea.
Any place can be any place before – open –– eyes. – seaside – anywhere.

ALEX: In the imagination, yes. Do you have a vivid imagination?

JUDITH: Imagination? No. None. How could I have?

ALEX: What do you mean?

JUDITH: – could a person with imagination feed their mother to the birds? – wouldn't make sense.

Short silence.

ALEX: Did you? Do that? Did you? Feed your mother to the birds?

JUDITH: Yes.

ALEX: Are you sure of this?

JUDITH: Well, yes.

ALEX: You remember doing this?

JUDITH: You think it's a thing one might forget?

ALEX: Do you know what you are saying?

JUDITH: – gulls. The gulls. –– –– always around and

around. Swooping down and soaring up up up. Because –
the cliff, well – – a sort of cliff 'cause – – cut like – cliff,
so straight, so high, so deep. – don't know how deep.
Hundreds – –– deep. – straight wall – red rock. Bushes
grow. Straight out – –. Purple. Long. Pendulous. Purple.
Blooms. Blooms.
Of course, –– pieces –– –– caught in – branches. Of
course, and – birds –– crash, crash on– – branches and.
Of course, some pieces –– –– dropped right down. All
the way down. –– must have done.

ALEX: They did, yes.

JUDITH: Yes.

ALEX: Some men working on the railway line at the
bottom.

JUDITH: Yes. All the way down there. – – –– another
world.

ALEX: Unfortunately perhaps, it is this world.

JUDITH: From above. – –– look down on– – tops of –
trees.
Perhaps.
Probably.
Yes.

ALEX: The pieces –

JUDITH: No. Don't talk –– that. – don't know how tired –
– – –. ––– no idea how often –– –– asked. – ––
nothing to say. –– – nothing to be said.

ALEX: But you've never said anything. You've never spoken
at all. You've been silent for seven months.

JUDITH: (*Without indignation.*) They've talked though. On
and on and on. They've never stopped. They can't give –
– rest. – makes – head hurt the way they go on.

The other women here. You'd think they'd have some sympathy a person loses her mother but no. —— —— terrible to me. Thinking I'd killed – mother and – . Horrible creatures. Worse than – gulls. Anyway that's – over –. – removed from them. – on my own now.

ALEX: Is that better? Is that more acceptable to you.

JUDITH: It's not better. It's more acceptable.

ALEX: You must want very much to get out of here.

JUDITH: (*Not uncheerfully.*) I don't mind. It's as good as anywhere now.

She cries silently. These tears are a physical nuisance. Unconnected with emotion.

ALEX leaves time for tears to stop. Short silence.

ALEX: Do you realise what you have said?
Do you wish me to wipe the tape?

JUDITH: Wipe?

ALEX: Erase.

JUDITH: My words?!

ALEX: Yes. Your words.

JUDITH: No! Why? What for?

ALEX: Don't you realise what you have said?
After seven months silence you have told me.
You've admitted to me that you killed your mother.

JUDITH: I said that?

ALEX: You admitted it. To this machine.

JUDITH: No?

ALEX: Yes.

JUDITH: I never said that. Never. I never said that?

Blackout.

In darkness on tape: fastwind gabble then, 'imagination feed their mother to the birds' etc.

Scene 18

Desk light snaps on.

ALEX stops the tape.

ALEX: And you're right, Judith. You did not say it. You did not say you killed your mother. There is no question. I've listened to the tape and listened to it. You did not say that. You said – merely – Ha – You fed your mother to the birds.

He switches to record.

Barratt –

He stops.

He takes the incriminating tape from the machine. Thinks. Puts it away in a drawer.

Puts a clean tape into the machine.

They want an assessment. I can't give it. Not yet. I need more time. Yes, she speaks. But only to me. At least, up to our last meeting this was the case; so I assume – (*To himself.*) Does she still remain silent when I'm not there?

Blackout.

In darkness:

JUDITH: Of course – –, yes. ––– no one else for talking.

Scene 19

The room.

ALEX at table.

JUDITH continuing speech (above) as lights come up.

JUDITH: (*Factual.*) A woman brings – breakfast and – other things. – –– Good morning Murderess. Good morning Motherkiller. – bangs the plates. – bangs the door. –– – big woman. They are big women. Well, –– have to be. – – – bosom like – Rock of Gibraltar.

ALEX: What do you do? When she talks to you in this way?

JUDITH: (*Looks at him.*)

ALEX: Well, you have said you don't speak. What do you do?

JUDITH: Sometimes - look at the wall. Sometimes – look at the window. – can't look out of it, –– too high. Sometimes I smile at her. It depends.

ALEX: On what? Does it depend.

JUDITH: Some days it's a good mood. I like to see her. Other days………

ALEX: Yes, I see.
You talked about your house. Moving there being a 'comedown.'

JUDITH: Oh yes.

ALEX: Where did you live before?

JUDITH: – Clifton before! Right by Saint Vincent Rocks! Right by – beautiful bridge. Right facing it. Absolutely! Do you know – up there?

ALEX: Yes of course I do.

JUDITH: You see there we had – real cliff. Up there, the birds – ! Oh my God you could fly. My God that was a proper cliff with a proper river at the bottom of it. A railway! What kind of a thing is that to have at the bottom of a cliff? They had to cut out that cliff for the railway I suppose, all the little railway men in those little railway houses up there.
But the river cut out our cliff.
Just by moving.
Through the rock.
Imagine that.

ALEX: When did you move from Clifton?

JUDITH: It was a lovely house. Curving windows. White. Little black balconies, oh yes.
I don't know. Three. Four.

ALEX: And why? Did you move.

JUDITH: My father.

ALEX: Your father?

JUDITH: Yes.

ALEX: He – died?

JUDITH: Died, went away. I don't know. We moved.

ALEX: You really don't know?

JUDITH: She never said.

ALEX: You never asked?

JUDITH: (*Sighs.*)

ALEX: It tires you to talk about this.

JUDITH: (*Factual.*) I was happy then I was unhappy. That's all.

ALEX: You were unhappy living with your mother there?

JUDITH: There, yes. With my mother, no. It's hard when you make two questions into one.

ALEX: I'm sorry.

JUDITH: (*Sighs.*)

ALEX: Are you tired now? Forgive me. All those years living with your mother. You never asked her where your father had gone?

JUDITH: (*Looks at him.*)

ALEX: Where did you think he had gone?

JUDITH: I supposed he must have died. I suppose. Maybe?

ALEX: Forgive me for tiring you.

JUDITH: When you mean unhappy, you say tired.

ALEX: Yes? Do I? Yes. I do. Why? Tired and unhappy. Why? Are they alike, do you think?

JUDITH: They're similar.
And that's not why.

ALEX: You're right. That's not why. I must not do it again.

JUDITH: Why? Mustn't you.

ALEX: It's dishonest.

JUDITH: I don't mind.

Silence.

ALEX: Why did you decide to talk to me?

Silence.

Were you tired?

He gives a small laugh because he has made her smile.

Silence.

JUDITH: You stopped being – the psychiatrist. And you weren't afraid.

ALEX: Not true, strictly.

JUDITH: Afraid, yes. But not of the monster. Only of – (*The word 'failure' hangs in the air but is not spoken.*) In case it wouldn't work. Do you see?

ALEX: Yes I see.

JUDITH: So I thought, why not?

ALEX: And are you? The monster?

JUDITH: I don't know that. What do you think?

ALEX: I don't know any better than you.

JUDITH: Well, that's something.

ALEX: Yes!

Silence.

Because she has been sad except when talking about Clifton and because this silence is a happier one, he goes on:

Were you ever happy, apart from the time you lived up by the suspension bridge? At any time since?
During any part of your life. Was there anything that brought happiness into your life? Ever? At any time?

Silence. Which hardens into a refusal to answer.

He risks:

You see, we found some letters.

JUDITH: Oh no oh no. Oh No. I knew I knew. Hide them, burn them! Why? Why didn't I? I knew, I knew! Ohhh.

Short silence.

Did you read my letters?

ALEX: Yes.

JUDITH: They are my letters!

ALEX: The police felt they had a right to take them.

JUDITH: The police?

ALEX: Barratt too. Doctor Barratt has copies.

JUDITH: Copies.
Nobody was to see them. They were never sent to anybody.

ALEX: No.

The exchange becomes increasingly chaotic, seamless. Her first spontaneous reaction perhaps ever.

JUDITH: Nobody was to see them.

ALEX: Who was Gerald?

JUDITH: Nobody.

ALEX: Is Gerald.

JUDITH: They are mine. My letters.

ALEX: Yes.

JUDITH: My lovely letters. They were in the drawer. I had a key.

ALEX: Did your mother see them?

JUDITH: No!

ALEX: How do you know?

JUDITH: I had the key. Ohhh. How did they get the key?

ALEX: Take your hands away from your face. Look at me.

He is gentle and quiet but doesn't let her off the hook:

Do you swear those letters were never sent?
Do you swear no one ever saw them?

JUDITH: I didn't think you were here for swearing. I didn't
think that was your particular function. I didn't think
that was where you were heading.

ALEX: Listen to me.

JUDITH: I said I have a problem with hearing.

ALEX: I don't think you are hearing my thoughts.

JUDITH: No because everything is flying around all over
the place, nothing will stay still, how can I hear
anything?

ALEX: You must let me tell you what my intentions are,
you must let me speak.

JUDITH: I mustn't must anything! I don't have any musts!

ALEX: Please?

JUDITH: I've started talking and now I can't stop. That's
what happens when you start something, you find
yourself going on with it whether you want to or not.
Talking was the most dangerous always. I knew. I knew.
Mmmmf. Mmmmf.

ALEX: Take your hand away.

JUDITH: Mmmmf, Mmmmf!

ALEX: (*Starts to laugh and goes on. Stops. Silence. Gentle,
light:*) Was Gerald real?

Did Gerald exist?

Was Gerald your father's name?

Take your hand away.
Please.
Let me see your mouth.

Did your mother dislike Gerald?
Did your mother like Gerald?
You say in one letter… 'Mother pours tea. Your hands are so big.'

When you cry like that making your hand all wet, does that make you happier? Not happier, I'm sorry. More peaceful, inside? Does it remind you of when you were a child? Of childhood sadness?

He pushes the packet of tissues towards her.

Do you wish to take one?
Would you like me to come and wipe your face?
Would you like Gerald to do that?

Silence. During which she makes it clear she has returned to silence where it was safer. And he realises he has taken the wrong approach.

I am more sorry than I can ever say.

A distant bell rings.

The key turns in the lock of the door.

Our time is up.

Light fades.

Scene 20

Lights up.

The room.

ALEX waits. He hasn't slept much.

She's late. Very late.

ALEX walks, sits, groans, stands. Puts his forehead against the window. Believes she is not going to come.

JUDITH comes into the room. Can't go to her window because he is there, so stands where she is, hardly in the room, but neutral. She too looks a little less neat. ALEX turns.

Silence.

ALEX: (*Considers things to say. Rejects them all.*) Today we have that rare thing – a blue sky.
There it is. I give it back to you.

He leaves the window. She stays where she is. There is no other indication of her state of mind.

You're angry with me.
You appear to be angry with me.
Are you? Angry with me?

JUDITH: (*Nothing.*)

ALEX: You should be. You should enthusiastically be angry with me, God help me, for my clumsy blundering.
I want to say 'Silence today. Silence for an hour,' but I can't. You've returned to a silence from which you were beginning to emerge and I do not like it. I don't like it at all. I don't want you to drop back into that black – And sink. I do not think you should go back there.

JUDITH: (*Looks at him.*)

ALEX: I believe there is something to be saved here, Judith. Something that should be saved.
I think you should believe that too.

JUDITH: (*Nothing.*)

ALEX: (*Moves around the room.*) ………Yes………

What a hideous piece of carpet this is.

………Yes………

He stops.

Yes.

Look, Judith.

Having come to a decision he is brisk. He challenges her:

Since you refuse to speak to me, I am going to tell you a story. Yes. It's a story that begins on just such a day as this. A bright day. Blue sky, fresh breeze. Some men are working on the railway line at the foot of a sheer rock railway cutting hundreds of feet deep. Perched on the top of this cutting a row of houses. Like teeth. Small elegant teeth. The men notice that there are more birds than usual about. Scores of seagulls, wheeling and pouncing at the rock and taking off again, food hanging from their beaks. The noise of the birds was deafening. One of the men was alarmed. He did not like birds. A rooted fear. He talked even of leaving the spot, asking to be transferred to a different job. A younger man mocked him. It was this man, the one who mocked, whose head was nearly brushed by the wings of a gull which flew close to him with a human hand in its beak. It was this man who fainted later because, having alarmed the bird by flailing his arms, it dropped the hand. Which had a wedding ring on it.

And that is how the search of the rock began and why the police visited you in your house at the top of the pseudo cliff. Your mother's name was etched inside the ring. When they called on you, you let them in. But you did not speak to them. That was seven months ago and you have not spoken since. To them or anyone else either. Except me.

Now my beginning of the story is not the real beginning of the story. Of course you know and I know that a story can begin anywhere. The true beginning of this story is so far back nobody could find it. But you could begin it before my beginning. And in a different place. Almost certainly not at the bottom of the cliff. Crypto-cliff. Up on the top inside the house for instance.

I told you I went inside the house. I liked it in there. Did you? It's a nice little house. You must miss it I should think. I've talked too much.

Can't you stop me. A vacuum will always be filled. Your silence is that. Sucking words out of me. You could put a stop to that.

Ah my dear, never mind. Let's turn this damn thing off.

He turns recorder off. Groaning and stretching he goes to the window.

Did you ever see a place with less of a view? A yard and another wall. Twelve empty windows in this wall. And eighteen inches of sky.

Short silence.

I saw a Monet the other day. Five poplars, a blue sky, clotted thick white clouds – ah – bulging through the trees. It was astonishing the way it made you feel.

A suddenly companionable silence.

JUDITH joins him. They stand side by side.

JUDITH: Gerald used to come and do the garden. I didn't ask him to come, he wanted to. The garden wall was high. You could only see over from upstairs. He made the hole, the window, in the wall to see right across, miles and miles. Trees and steeples. And down the rock. It was dizzying to look down the rock, I didn't do it often. Gerald...... Mother was small and I am thin with long narrow bones. He filled up the doorways and the room, he filled up the whole room and everything dwindled, everything around him went small. The chairs and the plates. The forks. You should have seen how small they were. The ceilings came very low and I used to think sometimes we shall all be crushed! I didn't mind, you know. I liked it. We might all be crushed all together by the walls and ceilings moving – in – and down and – in. Just Gerald would be there standing up and all the rest of us, chairs and people tiny round his feet, like little. Like little. Little tiny – caterpillars leaning backwards lifting up our heads. I used to laugh. I often used to laugh sitting with Gerald. Mother used to tell him I had always been odd and not to let it worry him.

ALEX: What did he say to that?

JUDITH: Say?

She laughs softly.

He smiled at me! I didn't smile back because Mother would have seen me and –
I used to smile in the garden. When I first saw him he was in the garden. I couldn't understand how he had got there. I looked up at the sky to see if he had fallen into the garden. That was his first smile. I wanted him to love me. I think he would have wanted to love me if he had known how but he didn't know how. He came to help mother with the garden. Mother never went out in the garden She never went out anywhere. She wasn't ill. She was ill but it was the not going out anywhere that was her illness. That was simply her illness.

ALEX: Did you try to persuade her to go out?

JUDITH: Why? People can stay in if they want to.

ALEX: When did she stop going out?

JUDITH: I never noticed that.

ALEX: You were still at school? You were still a schoolgirl?

JUDITH: I must have been.

ALEX: It must have been a constriction on you.

JUDITH: No.

ALEX: Judith!

JUDITH: When you call me Judith like that with such
passionate impatience, I think I could start to live again.
Just for a moment.

ALEX: Did Gerald say Judith like that?

JUDITH: (*Doesn't reply.*)

ALEX: Why Gerald?

JUDITH: Why not?

ALEX: He worked for a gardening firm? They sent him?

She looks at him for a moment.

JUDITH: No. He drew plans. Lovely gardens with shapes
and colours. The real garden was just hard earth. He got
spades and big – instruments – and broke it all up. All
that dusty yard with high walls, he broke it up. He was a
sort of earthquake. Ohhh.
He wore just trousers. Nothing else. Not in the street or
the house. In the garden. Sometimes I would touch his
back. Like that. With the flat of my hand. Because it was
shining. My hand would be wet and I would put my hand
to my face, flat like that. First on his back, then to my
face. And Gerald would smile. He had a habitually
solemn face but he smiled at me. With me. I hoped he
might love me but –

ALEX: Why Gerald?

JUDITH: I don't know. I never felt that before. There was
never a man in the house before. A man who filled up
the house like that and stood in the garden. Smiling.
Only smiling at me.

ALEX: I meant why Gerald to do the garden? Why him?
Why did your mother hire him?

JUDITH: Hire him? Smiling only at me. No.

ALEX: He was not hired? Then why did he come? Where from? Did he live close by? How did he and your mother meet? How did he manage to get into the house?

JUDITH: Once I went to the doorway without my clothes. The back door, that was. I stood in the doorway. I am not unsavoury without my clothes, though I am without surplus flesh. I waited. He did turn round. He was holding the spade. He looked at me. I was very happy. Gerald was happy. We stood for a long time. We didn't move. Then I went in. I put my clothes on and made the tea and Gerald put on his shirt and came in and we had tea and mother talked and Gerald went home. We were happy.

ALEX: Did you wish for anything more?

JUDITH: Yes.

ALEX: And Gerald?

JUDITH: For him it was everything. And I was very happy. I was also sad so I wrote my letters. For my secret's sake. I liked to write his name and how his back looked in the garden and how he – everything.

ALEX: When was this, Judith?

JUDITH: When? I don't know. Was it a long time ago? I have trouble knowing when things were.

ALEX: Or if they were?

JUDITH: Oh. You think I made Gerald up!

She is surprised.

In that case it would be mother who made him up because mother certainly saw him first.

ALEX: We can't ask her!

If your mother was agoraphobic –

JUDITH: (*Laughs. Another psychiatry word.*)

ALEX: If your mother did not look out of windows or go out of doors, how did she come to let this – to let Gerald in?

JUDITH: Tricks and traps. Did you say you were a psychiatrist? I have grave doubts.

She looked out of windows sometimes. She watched Gerald in the garden. No she couldn't see me when I took off my clothes and stood because I was in the doorway and you can't see the doorway from her window. It was the one place I couldn't be seen. It was clever of me to think of that, don't you agree? Do you admire my ingenuity? Normally I shouldn't think of such things but I would not have wanted to shock mother.

ALEX: What would your mother have done? If she had seen you?

JUDITH: So now you have decided to believe in the existence of Gerald for a while because you are thinking, (*Mocking his grand-guignol imaginings.*) her mother came wheeling in her chair behind naked Judith and shrieking she raised her stick and beat Judith, and Gerald though he was gentle became distressed and pushed past Judith who was crouching on the step and beat the mother with the spade and the mother died whoomf just like that from her heart which was not strong the slightest thing the slightest shock and then Judith had to think what to do because she could not allow Gerald to bear the burden though she needed his help and they cut the mother up with Gerald's saw which he had brought for cutting the beautiful trellis posts and she told Gerald to go and not to come back because it would be dangerous for him and he went away with all his implements including his saw naturally and she told him never to come back because oh yes I said that and he went away and he didn't come back and – And Judith made many heavy parcels and one by one she threw them to the birds. Of course because of the wall window that Gerald had made it would be easy to do that. I doubt that it would have been possible if the wall had retained its high solidity. Its solid height. This story is quite convincing except for certain melodramatic details – the stick, the wheelchair, the cripple beating her daughter, and he went away, and he didn't come back. Anyway………

Silence.

ALEX: The neighbours never saw Gerald.

JUDITH: Did they see the garden transformed? Did they see the terrace and the stone slabs and the Autumn crocuses? Did they see the trellis with the yellow roses and the crimson and the white and the clematis of all kinds including Nellie Moser and Vivian Pennell and the lavender and rosemary to be in grey leaf all the year round and the window in the wall to see so far? And the geraniums in urns? Who could have carried the urns? How did they think it was done? Did they think mother did all that? With her wheelchair and her stick? Did they think I did that with my job in a lawyer's office in Bedminster Parade?

ALEX: You stopped going to your job.

JUDITH: Yes because I wanted to be at the house when Gerald was there. (*Practical and simple.*) I didn't want to miss one moment of Gerald because you know things can last such a short time and never come back again and you mustn't waste the thing that is the most important thing. Only seeing Gerald once or twice as he arrived or departed. How could I carry on going to my job?

Silence.

ALEX: Why did Gerald not speak?

JUDITH: I said. He couldn't.

ALEX: Why? Couldn't he.

JUDITH: I don't know.

ALEX: He was – shy?
He was – mentally handicapped perhaps?

JUDITH: He was dumb. That's all.

ALEX: Dumb?

JUDITH: Yes.

ALEX: Literally dumb?

JUDITH: Verbally dumb.

Silence.

ALEX: Was he deaf also?

JUDITH: I don't know.

ALEX: You don't know?

JUDITH: He knew when I was there without looking and without my speaking. Always. How could I tell if he was deaf?

ALEX: Did he kill your mother?

JUDITH: I doubt it. My mother died.

ALEX: We know your mother died, Judith. We wouldn't be here now had your mother not died. The question is how did your mother die? When did she die? Why? You could clear this up. It could be over.

JUDITH: Over?

ALEX: It could be clear.

JUDITH: It could be clear?

Incredulous sad smile.

Lights fade.

In darkness on tape. ALEX's voice:

ALEX: There are two questions it seems to me.
Is she protecting Gerald?
Or has she invented him? To protect herself.

Scene 21

Lights up.

ALEX's desk.

He is drinking whisky but is not drunk.

He talks to recorder:

ALEX: Barratt, this is urgent.
They've got to find out if Gerald exists. Further questions must be asked. The right question must be asked. The right people must be asked the right question. If they won't do it, I'll do it myself. I'll go to every house. I'll question every person in the street.
If Gerald exists, it must be possible to find him. To question him.

He laughs.

He's dumb!

Blackout.

In darkness:

JUDITH: Oh Mamma Mamma talk to me!

Scene 22

Lights up.

The room.

JUDITH sitting. ALEX sitting.

JUDITH: Yes, Mamma talked to me.
  I once had a sweet little doll dears.
  Its hair was so charmingly curled.
  I woke mamma up, I put Mamma to bed, I told Mamma
  stories, I sang Mamma songs, I washed Mamma's hair
  and combed it and brushed it. I rolled it in curlers and I
  took the curlers out.
  I lost my poor little doll dears –

  I made Mamma's tea and I washed Mamma's plates. I
  wiped all the tables and the floors. I washed the lace
  curtains and put them back in the afternoon in case
  Mamma was looked upon. I read Mamma stories out of
  Pappa's books. They were beautiful books. We loved
  Pappa's books –
  I found my poor little doll dears.
  As I played in the heath one day.
  Her something was something something.
  And her curls were all washed away.

ALEX: You gave away one of the books to Betty in the
  office.

JUDITH: I gave her the Audubon. Was it the Audubon?
  Yes, it was flowers or birds. I can't remember which.
  Betty. She was a kind woman: a thing almost unique in
  nature, wouldn't you say?

ALEX: Your mother was not kind?

JUDITH She was my sweet little doll dears. How can a
  baby be kind?

ALEX: I didn't ask about a baby. I asked about your mother.

JUDITH: (*Sighs.*)

Silence.

ALEX: Where does this doll poem come from?

JUDITH: From Mamma.
My first song.

ALEX: Who was more important? Gerald or Mamma?

JUDITH: To me?
Oh Gerald was.

ALEX: So if it had come to a choice between Gerald and
Mamma, Gerald would have won?

JUDITH: Well naturally.

Especially when Mamma was dead.

ALEX: (*Controls himself.*)

JUDITH: Has Betty cut it up?

ALEX: (*Alert.*) What?

JUDITH: The book.
Did she do it with an electric saw?
Did she do it from hate? Or love?
Mother hated funerals. Funerals are public. You have to
be handled by strangers, carried out into the street.
Mother would have hated that.

Silence.

I'm really not too unhappy now.

ALEX: Without Gerald? Or Mamma?

JUDITH: I hope none of them recalls seeing Gerald in their
shrivelled little street. It's a pretty street, isn't it? I'm

sure you thought that. Though you wouldn't have imagined it so from my description. Am I hearing your thoughts?

That's a bad sign

Yes, you're beginning to shrink. That's a very bad sign. My telescope must have turned round.

People do get smaller. Mister Blake.
It happened very fast with Mister Blake. Zoomf! Just like that. Simply sucked down to the bottom of the well.
Zoomf! Very clear but tiny. As fast as a fall.
Surprising.
You can do it on purpose of course too.

ALEX: Cheryl?

JUDITH: Cheryl.

Silence.

ALEX: (*Looks at her. A long look. She is drifting away. A boat he has launched on the sea. He recognises the signs, feels the customary sense of achievement and regret. He rouses himself from the look.*) I may have some news for you. After the weekend.

JUDITH: For me? News? Oh well. I shall wait.

Blackout.

Scene 23

Lights up.

ALEX at his desk reading through his report.

He is opening a can of beans.

He is not entirely sober.

The can opener slips.

ALEX: Ach – a – damn.

Beans slide out onto his papers.

Ach. Christ. Ach. No.

He pathetically tries to mop his papers, save his report. Realises this is a hopeless task. Screws up the papers and throws them into the waste paper basket. Enraged at having lost his report, he throws the beans away also. And then even the can opener.

Yes. Well.
Three large whiskies is no basis for a report like this.
Three? Four, let's call a spade a spade. The very mention
of a spade and that huge bastard is standing in that
garden and she's –
Oh my God.

Well, well. Fancy. How about that? Hello Counter-
transference my old friend.

He pours a drink.

Six. Five.

He drinks.

The psychiatrist's psychiatrist. The cup that reveals.
Myself to myself. Cheers. Thanks.

He drinks.

Well, I certainly spilled the beans just there.

He laughs.

Hey, Barratt? Children. So simple. But she too. Is only a.
Is an only. Child. Tell you what. I'm going to wipe this
tape. 'Wipe? My words?' I'd die for her.

Perhaps Gerald would die for her.

Maybe her mother did.

I loathe her mother. I loathe Gerald.

God how I loathe Gerald.

He is getting up as the lights fade.

Scene 24

ALEX enters the room swiftly as the lights come up.

ALEX: They've found him.

They've found Gerald.

Nothing to say?

They asked at every house. Every one. 'Do you remember a very large man? With gardening tools? A van perhaps?' 'No, officer, no one like that, no.' No one remembered him, anyone like him. Then comes a keen young copper. Oh you'd like him, he's like an eel, shiny skin, sparkling teeth. 'What about a milkman?' he says to the lady opposite. You remember this lady? Grey hair squashed under a net, floral gown, plump pink folded arms on which she rests her big soft bosom? 'What about a postman? Or a man delivering papers? The man who reads the meter, what about him?, 'Ah!' says the grey-haired lady lifting her little pink hands, letting the bosom fall loose, 'Now you mention it!' And she says – Well what does she say, Judith? You know! You can tell me precisely what she said. You could have told us this months ago. You could have told me! Well, what did she say?

They come and go, don't they? Window cleaners. They appear, they disappear, they take their money in cash, no one knows their name, no one looks at them. In fact you could say everyone is busy keeping out of their sight. It is they who might look. Look in. Look on.

Did they have a van? There were two of them apparently. At first. Then one of them dropped out. The bosomy lady doesn't recall – was there a van? A van would have been useful you see. When Gerald too gave up the window business to concentrate on you. On your garden. A van would be useful for the tools. It's too long ago for anyone to recall. Isn't that sad?

Why didn't you tell me, Judith?

But apparently he wasn't all that big. Gerald. He wasn't all that big.

They all remember the window cleaners now. There were two of them, the silent one larger than the other, but neither of them particularly big.

Did you imagine that he was big? Or did you say that to put us off his scent?

Oh, Judith.

Will you turn round?

Will you look at me?

Please?

Silence.

She does not turn.

I am very sorry that Gerald's existence has been established.

I am very sorry.

Judith?

He walks about. Then sits. Perhaps on the edge of the desk.

I got drunk on Friday night. I'm not used to that. I still don't feel any too bright as a matter of fact. I ought not to speak about myself, it's just –

JUDITH: (*Turns.*)

ALEX: Ah?
  You look ill.

  Please sit down. Will you? You look – Please sit down,
  I'm afraid you might –

JUDITH: (*Whispers something.*)

ALEX: What? Would you like some water?
  Why do you smile?
  You asked for water?! I read your thoughts?!
  Here.

  He gets water.

  There, you see, you're not the only one.
  There.
  But won't you sit down?

JUDITH: (*Whispers.*)

ALEX: What?

JUDITH: (*Almost voiceless, as she remains throughout this section
  of the scene.*) They told me.

ALEX: Who told you? When? How could they have told
  you? They assured me I would be the first. They
  promised me. How did they tell you? Who?

JUDITH: The Rock of Gibraltar. I didn't know when. It was
  evening. It wasn't today. More water please.

ALEX: How could she know?

JUDITH: 'They've got him,' she said. 'They'll get it out of
  him.' Thank you.

  Silence. She drinks.

ALEX: They haven't got him, Judith.

JUDITH: What?

ALEX: No.

JUDITH: Ah!

ALEX: Never mind. It's not broken. Only spilt. You're all wet.

JUDITH: Don't touch me.

ALEX: No of course. Some tissues. Would you like me to fetch someone to –

JUDITH: Oh no!

Silence.

ALEX moves about, picking up glass. JUDITH mops her skirt.

ALEX: You don't like to be touched?
Well, of course you don't, how could you?
Is that what happened, possibly? Gerald tried to touch you? You became frantic, screamed perhaps? Your mother came to your aid, to save you from Gerald? Inadvertently she became the victim? An accidental death, in fact? Is that what happened, Judith? Something like that?

Silence.

JUDITH: They have not found him? Is that what you said?

ALEX: That's what I said.

JUDITH: Is it true?

ALEX: It's true.

JUDITH: Why not? Why haven't they?

ALEX: No records. No name. Not even an agreed description. Not a big man even. Especially. You see? A chap who came to clean the windows some months ago.

He has not been found.

I wasn't supposed to tell you that.

The woman who told you. Would you like me to register a complaint?

No.

Silence.

JUDITH in her own world.

ALEX, aware that she is on the brink of deep disclosure, appears lost in thought.

JUDITH: (*Still almost voiceless.*) My skirt's not too wet.

ALEX: No. No?

JUDITH: No.

ALEX: You've made it better now.

JUDITH: (*Recites like a child:*)
I once had a sweet little doll dears.
The prettiest doll in the world.
Her cheeks were so red and so white dears.
And her hair was so charmingly curled.
I lost my poor little doll dears
As I played in the heath one day.
I searched for her more than a week dears.
But I never could find where she lay.

She sighs deeply.

I found my poor little doll dears
As I played in the heath one day.
Folks say she is terribly changed dears,
For her paint is all washed away,
Her arm trodden off by the cows dears,
And her hair not the least bit curled –

She 'wakes'. Cries heartbrokenly.

He gives her time but not too much.

ALEX: Only her arm was not trodden off by the cows. Was it, Judith?

JUDITH: What does it matter? It's done.

ALEX: But how was it dome? Why was it done? By whom was it done? These things matter. Even to you.

JUDITH: I found my poor little doll……
That's all I know.
And whatever was done and how and by whom, it was my fault. It was. It was.

ALEX: (*After a little time.*) And do you want to live?

JUDITH: How?

ALEX: That's the question, yes.
We're here to answer it.

Silence.

He may move about.

To give her time:

To lighten her guilt:

Judith, if I declare you of unsound mind, you are likely to be locked away. Forever, virtually. People do not consider it normal to chop up your mother and feed her to the birds. Though of course there exist civilisations that feed their dead relatives to the vultures without the chopping up. They present the dainty dish in just one piece. There are those, too, who put their mums on bonfires, though were you to follow their example in your own backyard – no matter how improved by the incomparable Gerald – they would think it more than a little odd. Yes, even those who roast their mums alive.

It's the idea of doing it at home that strikes people as unseemly. Without benefit of clergy as it were. Even those who would declare that your home was your castle would most emphatically not approve. Doing it in the living room.

Where did you do it, by the way? The sawing up and parcelling. They found no trace.

Kitchen or bathroom would be the obvious choice, but it was done in neither of those places. As far as they can tell.

And the garden would be too public, wouldn't it? Even though your neighbours appear never to have looked out.

Can you look into the mists of –

JUDITH: Mists…… Yes……

I am inside a mirror.

It is a distortion mirror.

There are six Judiths, Geralds. Six or eight.

It is quite dark. Shadowy.

ALEX: Is that where you did it? In Gerald's van?

JUDITH: Gerald's van is blue. A beautiful blue. Like cornflowers. There are no words on the van. And no words inside the van! Because we do not speak!

ALEX: Is Gerald as big in the van as he had been in the house? Does the mirror turn your telescope around?

JUDITH: YES! Telescope! You! Yes! And Gerald. Gerald. Only once. Once once only once. Only once, please yes. Yes yes yes. Mamma, no! Gerald, no! Small, small, smaller, small, so tiny. Dot dot no! Dot dot dot don't don't don't Gerald don't. No! Mamma Mamma doll! Yet for old sakes' sakes she is still dears THE PRETTIEST DOLL IN THE WORLD!

She may try to mend 'broken doll'.

She moans quietly now and then, rocking.

ALEX: (*Gives her time but not too much. He pours some water. Quietly:*) Drink some water now.

JUDITH: (*A bright fast sweet chatter.*) Thank you, yes. Just a little milk. These are the prettiest porcelain cups. The tea tastes better, doesn't it? The cup makes all the difference. Take no notice of Judith, she's always been odd. She disappeared you know and we thought she had fallen down the gorge. Or even off the bridge, she was so fascinated by both those things you see. The cliff and the bridge. And you see a child's body was found. In the river, yes. They came to tell us and my husband had to go and see. He said Yes, that seems to be Judith, my daughter Judith who was four years old and was wearing a blue dress cornflower blue. And then he came home and when he turned the corner there she was! She ran to him and he fell down dead. In the street outside the house. With all the neighbours looking and such a fuss. And she doesn't remember. Doesn't remember him! Isn't it strange? She killed him really and she doesn't remember him at all. Who, Mummy? Daddy? Oh no I don't remember him! Now don't you agree, Gerald? Isn't that odd?

Coming back to herself, her voice trails off to a slow mumble.

But – she's been – ve-ry go-od t-o m-ee – – – –

Silence.

She is like a medium coming out of deep trance.

He gives her time.

ALEX: Drink some water, Judith.

When she speaks it is as though she is coming up from a dark well. Clear. Like water.

67

JUDITH: Yes.
Thank you.

She drinks deep.

She begins to look at the room, as though it is the first time she has seen it. She is drained, quiet, purified.

She looks at ALEX, seeing him for the first time perhaps.

Are you well? You don't look very well today.

ALEX: I have a little hangover. Apart from that – my own fault entirely – I am quite well. Thanks.

Silence.

JUDITH walks about.

Still in the drained exhaustion of one recently raised from the dead:

JUDITH: This room is worse than my cell you know.

ALEX: How? In what way?

JUDITH: This hideous carpet, these clashing colours. In my cell everything is plain. That's important to me. Mother liked pretty things. Patterned things. I don't know why, but I never did.

Silence.

She drinks.

I made Gerald do it.

ALEX: You made Gerald do it?

JUDITH: Yes

ALEX: Gerald was in your power?

JUDITH: Power! Yes! That was it! I made him – come into my power!

ALEX: How did you do that? It can't have been easy?

JUDITH: Easy!? No, it was hard! Harder than disappearing – someone.

She looks at him.

ALEX: Father? You had to disappear your father?

JUDITH: (*Weeping.*) I'd never do that again. Terrible. You've no idea.

She recovers. She speaks almost shyly, yet needing to communicate, to tell someone. For the first time in her life perhaps.

See, with Gerald – Well. What shall I say?
Have you ever known? When all life comes in just to you, like light, in your skin, and everything is alive, even chairs and tables and plates and forks, and you can feel all the life in everything and not just now but from the very beginning and not just how but why. You know why. You know the reason – These words are no good, words – are – no – good – But the reason was Joy. So much joy, it had to make life. And that's why life is so – – – – – – Ohhh.

Gerald felt also like that. But Gerald knew it was enough. Enough? Well, heavens, it was already too much. I had to leave my job because I was becoming able to be aware only of the light pulsing out of the walls, and the chairs expressing their boundless happiness. I couldn't be contained in there. Mister Blake was sad. I was sad but there was nothing else to be done. Someone said in the street, What are –
Someone said in the street, Are you looking for somewhere? And I said, No I'm just looking! And I was. Oh it was magnificent.
I don't know why I couldn't leave it as it was. Gerald was wise. People without words are wiser. Look at the mess I

made. And look at the fool I am making now. I'm
making the fool. I was wiser when silent.
(*She looks at him.*) You know.
And so – Ohhh – – – – – –

Silence.

Say something.

ALEX: I?

JUDITH: Yes. Say something to me.

ALEX: What shall I say?

JUDITH: What you are thinking.

ALEX: Can't you hear my thoughts?

JUDITH: I'm too full of my own.
Say.

ALEX: Ah. Well. That I love you, but that –

JUDITH: Yes! That's what I wanted you see. Gerald
couldn't speak – – – – – –
So – – – – – –

ALEX: I know you are not a virgin. They told me that. It's
in the reports.

JUDITH: Oh yes.
I made him come to me. I was in such a passion it
couldn't be contained. I was in a passion for taking off
my clothes! I wanted both of us to have no clothes. I
can't tell you how beautiful I knew that would be. And
Gerald was of a modest disposition. He so much didn't
want to – to – to come any closer to me. It was the
happiness that threw me. Drew me. Everything seemed
so light, so right, so – sensible, nothing could possibly
go wrong, be wrong. So I made him come with me, I
made him.

ALEX: You can draw a horse to water, Judith, but you can't –

JUDITH: Oh you don't know!

ALEX: But this was a large man, a largish man. You can't –

JUDITH: Oh yes! You can! You can. I was naked in the doorway and I simply tightened the – thread, whatever it is, the – twine. I made one step backwards down the hall. And Gerald made one step forwards, across the terrace he had made. And I made another step backwards, and he made another step forwards, and so on and so on. And I was so afraid, so frightened and so full of joy. And the power, you see. What you said. Just that. But I didn't know. And Gerald knew that he could not do that without making terrible grief. He knew and I should have believed in his wisdom and left him to be. Ohhhhh.
And we were in the living room and I was in such joy you've no idea. And we were on the floor and I wasn't even afraid. There was none of me left over to be afraid with. And it was not yet teatime but mother came into the room and Gerald leapt up like a – Oh the ceilings and floors and walls all met. Nothing could contain him. No room built by man.

And I don't know what happened after that. Not at all. Only, the doll was broken.
And if it hadn't been Mother it would have been me.
And I would have been glad for it to have been me.
Only who would then have looked after Mother?

Silence.

ALEX: Gerald, perhaps.

JUDITH: My little Mamma-doll.

And anyway Gerald couldn't come back again after that. Could he?
You see?

71

ALEX: (*Whispers.*) No.

JUDITH: I think Mamma just died. Like Father was said to have done. Like Father did. At the unexpected sight of me. Isn't that odd? It's – fitting. Don't you think?

But they'll never find Gerald.
Will they?
Do you think?

She laughs.

I let him in first. Not Mother. She said, There's a new window cleaner, Judith. He's shy. He doesn't look in like the other one. Then she said, The new window cleaner can't speak. He's not shy, dear, he's dumb.
And she laughed.
He made her happy. Isn't that odd? it's odd for someone to have that capacity. To make people happy. Not by saying. Or doing. Just by being. Isn't that odd?
He came to fill his bucket. I was at home because I had a cold. My nose was red. I let him understand that he might clean the back windows also. I brought him a cup of tea at the foot of his ladder out in the garden. He looked at the garden while he drank the tea. He did not look at me. I've never liked people to look at me so it was a shock to me to be made to feel lonely because he did not look. Imagine feeling jealous of a garden because he looked at it and not at you. I was jealous of the garden! That's when I must have decided to make him lift his eyes from the garden and turn and look at me. I must have decided it then, I think. I must have decided it then because I gave him a key. Yes! So that the next time he came he could come straight in and fill his bucket, it was a zinc bucket, a shiny one. And put his ladder up against the house and clean the windows at the back, even of Mother's room where she sat until teatime every day. And I came home quickly the next time and he was

there in the garden and that was the time that I looked
up to see if he had fallen from the sky and that was the
first time that his sad face smiled. So you see.
And the next time he had his – implements – and he was
making the hole in the wall.
And that's how it began.

Silence.

ALEX: I see.

JUDITH: (*Wistful.*) Do you?
I can't see, really. Not in the least.
I can't see the plan.

Did I tell you Gerald brought plans? Lovely colours and
shapes.
But no details.
The details were in the garden itself.
When it was made.
Not before.
Do you see?

Silence.

And the next thing I remember is being in the van in the
dimness of the light with Gerald and poor little doll and
seeing us all distorted in the greyish silver dark.

She covers her face with her hands for a moment.

She may get up and move about.

At least my cell is not a distorting mirror, you see.
At least it's not that.

Did you say your name was Alec?

ALEX: (*A moment.*) Alex.

JUDITH: Oh yes. I'm sorry not to remember your name.
I have had other things – pressing – on my mind.

ALEX: Yes.

JUDITH: So you see, I shan't mind being kept in a cell. Not really. As long as they don't keep me in a place where there are many patterns and colours. I like only to have things plain. Could you ask them that for me?

ALEX: I'll do my best.

JUDITH: Thank you.
Thank you very much.

ALEX: (*Coughs or similar strangled noise.*)

Silence.

JUDITH: What shall I do there?

ALEX: Well. I suppose, books, and –

JUDITH: Without Gerald.
They'll never find Gerald for me.
What shall I do without Gerald?

ALEX: Yes.

Silence.

I could come and see you there.

JUDITH: You?

ALEX: Yes.

JUDITH: Oh.

Silence.

She considers this. Looks out of the window.

ALEX: What are you seeing out of the window now?

Silence.

Trees?

Silence. They both slightly smile.

JUDITH: Will you turn it off now?

ALEX: What?
   Oh! This?

JUDITH: And then I'll tell you what I see.

ALEX: Yes.

He turns off the machine.

Silence.

Lights fade.